All About Math Symbols

Written by Nancy Kelly Allen

Rourke
Educational Media

rourkeeducationalmedia.com

Scan for Related Titles
and Teacher Resources

www.rourkeeducationalmedia.com

PHOTO CREDITS: Cover: © Joshua Hodge Photography, Kudryashka; Page 1: © Shironosov; Page 3: © eulerlagrange, boygovideo; Page 5: © Ankevanwyk; Page 7: © Dantok; Page 9: © 18percentgrey; Page 10: © Elenathewise; Page 11: © Samgrandy; Page 12: © logoboom; Page 13: © Frank-Boston; Page 14: © bebo; Page 15: © ajafoto, bmcent1, matt_benolt, Pyp2010ha; Page 20, 21: © GlobalP; Page 22: © WestLight

Edited by Jill Sherman

Cover and Interior design by Tara Raymo

Library of Congress PCN Data

All About Math Symbols / Nancy Kelly Allen
(Little World Math)
ISBN 978-1-62169-891-3 (hard cover)
ISBN 978-1-62169-786-2 (soft cover)
ISBN 978-1-62169-990-3 (e-Book)
Library of Congress Control Number: 2013936808

Also Available as:

Rourke Educational Media
Printed in the United States of America,
North Mankato, Minnesota

Rourke
Educational Media

rourkeeducationalmedia.com

customerservice@rourkeeducationalmedia.com • PO Box 643328 Vero Beach, Florida 32964

We use signs every day. A math sign is called a symbol.

Symbols stand for things that can be counted or measured.

A number is a symbol that tells an amount.

How many can you count?

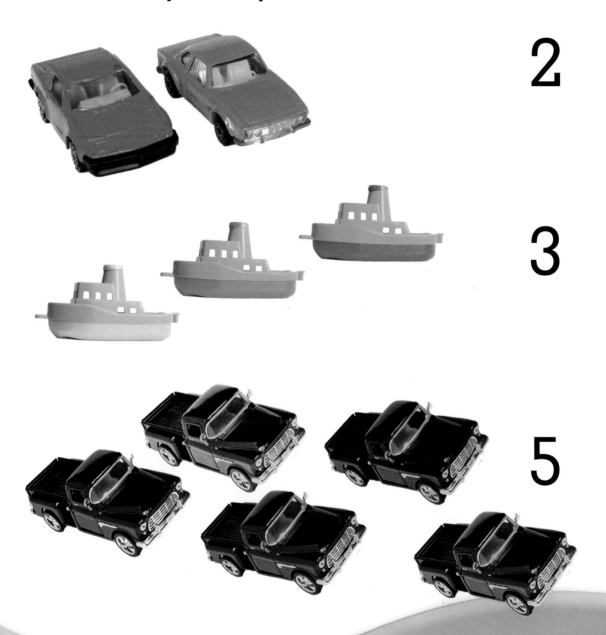

2

3

5

The plus symbol means add.

Add the number of robots.

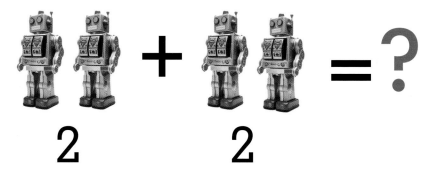

2 + 2 = ?

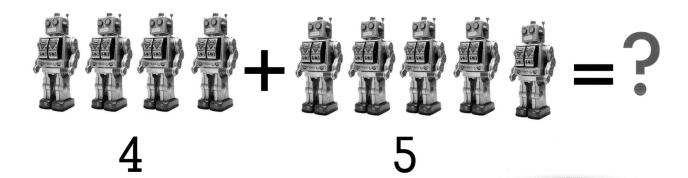

4 + 2 = ?

4 + 5 = ?

The minus symbol means subtract or take away.

How many cookies are left?

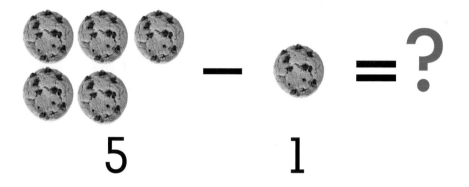

5 − 1 = ?

8 − 2 = ?

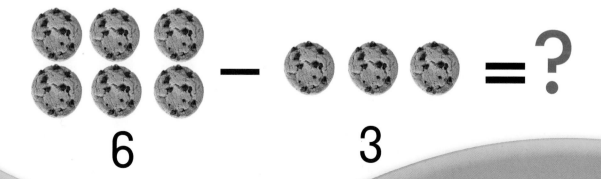

6 − 3 = ?

The equal symbol means the same as.

Do the trucks equal the same number?

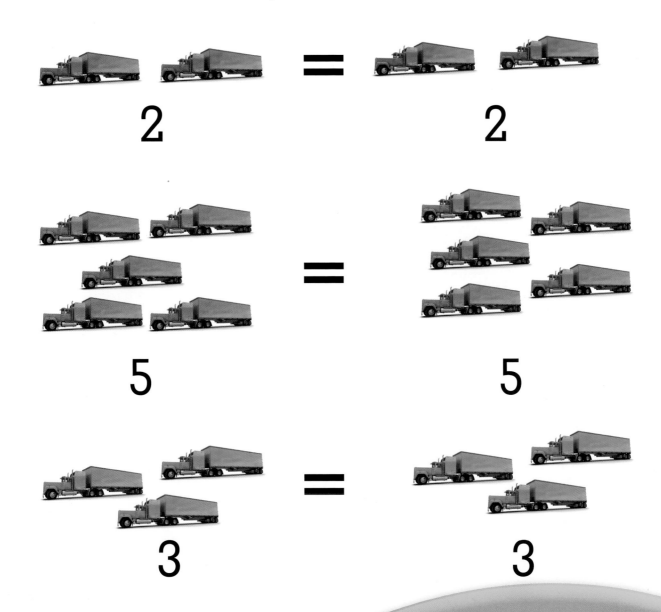

2 = 2

5 = 5

3 = 3

The degree symbol measures temperature.

Which is hotter? The ice cream or the hot chocolate?

20°F   200°F

Which is cooler? The pizza or the soup?

85°F

90°F

The dollar symbol and the cents symbol measure money.

The dollar symbol measures one dollar and more. The cents symbol measures less than one dollar.

Which is more?

$3.00 or 30¢?

$5.00 or 75¢?

Which is less?

$1.50 or 50¢?

$ 2.25 or 25¢?

The greater than symbol shows that one number is bigger than another.

The greater than symbol is like a hungry alligator. The open mouth faces the bigger number.

Which number is greater?

$$6 > 3$$

$$5 < 7$$

$$8 < 9$$

The less than symbol shows that one number is smaller than another.

Which number is less?

2 < 5

1 < 4

5 > 3

Math symbols help us count
and measure.

Can you find the correct symbol?

$$7 \; (+ \text{ or } -) \; 1 = 6$$

$$3 \; (+ \text{ or } -) \; 2 = 5$$

$$1 + 3 \; (<, =, >) \; 4$$

$$5 \; (< \text{ or } >) \; 2$$

$$2 \; (< \text{ or } >) \; 3$$

Index

Websites

www.kidsnumbers.com
www.funbrain.com/brain/MathBrain/MathBrain.html
www.bbc.co.uk/bitesize/ks1

About the Author

Nancy Kelly Allen lives in Hazard, Kentucky, with her husband and two dogs. The dogs wag their tails when Nancy comes home each day. They give her sloppy kisses, too. Wags and kisses are symbols that the dogs are happy to see her. Wags + Kisses = Happy!

Meet The Author!
www.meetREMauthors.com